The Second

Book

*More thoughts, stories and happenings
in the life of one of America's
great storytellers and motivational speakers.*

by
Riney Jordan

The Second Book

ISBN # ISBN-13: 978-1484183175
ISBN-10: 1484183177

Printed in the United States of America

First Edition, June, 2013

Riney Jordan Company
387 County Road 220
Hamilton, TX 76531
254-386-4769

Email: **riney@yahoo.com**
www.rineyjordan.com

DEDICATION

To
My unbelievable wife

Karen

"Her children arise and call her blessed; her husband also, and he praises her."

Proverbs 31:28

Table of Contents

*"Let's see … I've got the first book,
'All the Difference,'
… now what would be a good name for
the second book?*

H-m-m-m.

OK. 'The Second Book' it is!"

CHAPTER
ONE

"A Day Little William

Will Never Forget"

"Some choices we live not only once but a thousand times over, remembering them for the rest of our lives."

--Richard Bach

A Day Little William Will Never Forget

When my little great-nephew William started to kindergarten, we all held our breath. Oh, so full of energy, and always busy;.

Yep. William had grown into an energetic, enthusiastic, extremely active five-year-old.

For years, he has kept us entertained and given us plenty of stories to tell again and again.

For example, when he was only a couple of years old, the church that he and his family attended was located right behind his house. Only a fence with a gate kept him at home. But one day someone forget to lock the gate, and our little William went through the gate and headed for the front doors of the church, just a couple of hundred feet away.

The only real problem with this was that William decided it was entirely too warm that day to wear clothes, so just before going through the gate, he shed them. Every piece of them!

He walked proudly up to the glass doors, began hitting them with his fist, and the noise attracted the interest of the church secretary, who got up from her desk to check it out.

Well, it's not everyday that you have a church member show up the way God sent him down here in the first place.

But, someone immediately found some "swaddling" clothes, wrapped him up, gave mom a call, and all's well that ends well.

The gate has been permanently sealed since the incident and, to our knowledge, no other totally unclothed person has ever been on the front porch of that Baptist church.

William has always been fascinated by swords, spears, knives, etc. If there's a swash-buckling movie on television, William is right there, watching every move. And then, when the movie is over, he duplicates the sword fight with anything he can find.

Oh, yes. The light sabers from Star Wars were a must for William. He carried his saber around with him all the time. Many hanging baskets and small shrubs have been on the receiving end of William's wrath.

For example, take his grandmother's gorgeous hanging basket. Here it was, in all its beauty, on the back patio of her home. Well, when William walked out and saw those gorgeous ivy vines hanging there, it was as if they said, "I dare you to swing at me with that light saber."

And, of course, he did. Leaves and tendrils went flying

everywhere. And, because he was always "whacking" something with a sword or saber, the family immediately named him "William the Whacker."

Well, "William the Whacker" started kindergarten that year. We were all prepared for stories of his battling the teacher with a yardstick, or pinning some child to the bulletin board, and thus, learning where the principal's office was on that first day.

And, like any little child who loves to play, going to kindergarten on a daily basis was *not* at the top of his list of ways to spend the day.

The delivery to school that morning went fairly well. William immediately spotted his best little friend who was wailing at the top of his lungs. "William the Whacker" looked back at his mom with a message that read: "Do I *have* to go in there?"

So, when school was dismissed, we were all anxiously awaiting the report on our little William. We were certain that there were going to be some negative responses.

It seems that when his mom appeared outside the classroom door that afternoon, William was out in the hall in a bound.

With a smile that would forever be etched into his mother's brain, William's eyes grew wide with excitement. They were sparkling like a 10-carat diamond. His fists were clinched together as if he could barely restrain himself.

"Mom, Mom!" he shouted.

The mom knelt down, expecting to hear the worst.

"Mom," he repeated. "I have just had the GREATEST DAY OF MY ENTIRE LIFE!"

Wow! Does it get any better?

So, when you read the critical articles in newspapers and magazines about our public schools... when you see the negative reports on television ... when you hear the grumblings of folks who simply don't have the slightest idea what's happening on a daily basis in our public schools, remember "William the Whacker."

He's just a normal five-year-old kid who surprisingly discovered that school can be one of the best things that has ever happened to him.

And, I would go to the stake defending the belief that there are countless thousands more just like him.

We're so proud of you, "William the Whacker"... and that kindergarten teacher is truly a miracle worker!

CHAPTER TWO

"A Lesson on Teaching a Child to Say His Name"

"It's always helpful to learn from your mistakes because then your mistakes seem worthwhile."

-- Garry Marshall

"A Lesson on Teaching a Child to Say His Name"

My friend of over forty years is Dr. Paul Jennings. When I first met Paul he was a speech therapist who loved kids and thoroughly enjoyed his work.

Paul tells a great story about one of his first students. The records showed that little Raymond was six years old and desperately needed the help of a speech therapist.

The first day Raymond came to class, Paul immediately recognized that he had a tremendous difficulty with the sound of "R." In fact, when you asked him his name, he simply said, "Waymon."

"We've got to correct this," Paul told his classroom teacher. "I'll have him sounding those "R's" in nothing flat."

Well, for weeks, Paul worked with Raymond to get that "R" sound at the beginning of his name.

"R-r-r-r-r-r," Paul would say. "Look in the mirror with me. Make your mouth the same shape as mine. I know you can do it. Keep trying."

Eventually, he could say "Raymond" almost as clearly as Paul could say it.

"Now, when anyone asks you your name, you just remember what we've learned and say 'Raymond' as clearly as you can."

Oh, the feeling of success in the classroom! The sheer joy of realizing that you've made a difference in the life of a child! That break-through when only weeks before it had seemed almost impossible!

But, here it was. Raymond had learned from the best of them.

That spring, during the school's open house, Paul met Raymond's parents for the first time. Clearly, they had no speech problems, Paul noticed as they introduced themselves to him.

"It's a pleasure to meet you," they said. Our little boy really enjoys your class."

"Oh, I enjoy him as well," Paul responded. "We had a little difficulty at first with the "R" sound, but he's got it down pat now."

"Very good," his mother said. "Waymond will see you on Monday."

"Uh, what did you say," Paul questioned.

"I said that Waymond will see you Monday for your speech class."

"But you called him 'Waymond,' Paul said. "His name's not 'Raymond?'"

"Why no," she answered.

"Oh, goodness," Paul said as his face began to turn beet red. "I've been working for weeks to get him to make that "R" sound on the front of his name."

"Well, that explains why he's been calling himself 'Raymond' every time he meets someone. Do you mind working with him to go back to 'Waymond?'"

"Not at all," Paul said. "We'll begin work on undoing my mistake first thing Monday morning."

Oh, no one ever said that we were perfect, but now and then it's good to admit it, and then laugh at ourselves when we make a mistake.

It's also refreshing to laugh at those things that invariably happen in every classroom.

Let me relate a couple that have been told to me as I travel and speak to teachers all over the country.

I'll never forget the time a teacher told me about taking her first grade students to the bathroom. She introduced her next lesson and the students immediately began to work on the assignment.

One of the boys in the class walked up to the desk and asked if he could go to the bathroom.

"But we just got back from the bathroom," she answered.

"I know, teacher," he said. "But that time I had to stand up and this time I have to sit down."

For as John Powell is credited with saying, ""Blessed is he who has learned to laugh at himself, for he shall never cease to be entertained."

CHAPTER THREE

"The Story of Randy: Another Casualty in the War on Drugs"

"In the long run, we shape our lives, and we shape ourselves. The process never ends until we die. And the choices we make are ultimately our own responsibility."

-- Eleanor Roosevelt

"The Story of Randy: Another Casualty in the War on Drugs"

As a former teacher, I always appreciated those students who were well-mannered, who did their assignments without a struggle, and who always had a smile on their face. Oh, yes. They *do* exist! There may not be as many as there used to be…but there are still countless numbers of students out there who don't "stand out" simply because they're not breaking the rules. They do what is expected. And they're not constantly demanding attention.

John Greenleaf Whittier once wrote: "For of all sad words of tongue or pen, the saddest are these: 'It might have been!'"

Oh, such is the case of a young boy we'll call Randy. This is a true story that has not yet seen its final chapter. He came to school regularly. He was always pleasant to teachers and other students. He always had a gentle smile on his face. He also had a great many interests. He seemed to love music and played the violin for a while. When he was in middle school, he joined the band. Randy was quite good on the trumpet.

He also loved animals of all kinds. In a pet store, he seemed to shine. He was drawn to dogs and cats and fish and lizards and rodents. His room became a menagerie filled with aquariums and cages.

And while he wasn't one of the top students, his grades were what many would call "average." He didn't smoke. He didn't drink. His leisure time was spent playing video games, caring for his pets, and being with friends who had interests similar to his.

Yes, Randy was one of those students who often gets overlooked because they "blend in" so easily. And, perhaps it was for this reason that many of us didn't see the changes that were happening in his young life.

At seventeen, like most boys that age, he wanted a car. A part-time job at a pizza parlor late in his senior year solved that problem. Almost overnight, Randy became a different person.

His grades dropped. His friends changed. His attitude plummeted.

One day his parents received a letter from the school telling them of the consequences if his attendance didn't improve. As it turns out, he had been leaving home in the morning for school, but would actually spend his day wandering around in the mall or driving aimlessly for hours.

Immediately upon graduation, he "declared" his independence. He wanted more freedom. He stayed out later and later. Cigarettes and alcohol became evident. And this child, who would never have been described as rebellious, was suddenly rebellion's poster child. Although the parents knew something was dramatically different about Randy, they attributed much of it to a "phase" he was going through, much like all of us feel at eighteen years of age.

Before the parents could seriously analyze their son's sudden and noticeable personality change, several major events took place. First, the father was seriously injured in an automobile accident a couple of hours from home. The wife immediately drove to the hospital to be with him. That weekend, their home was burglarized. Electronic equipment, guns, jewelry and other valuables were stolen. Police and parents were baffled.

Then, a few weeks later, the parents received a late-night phone. It was Randy, calling to tell them that he was in jail.

As it turned out, he and a group of about fifteen other young men had been burglarizing homes for the past several months. The reason: to get money for drugs. He would later admit that he had been responsible for the burglary of his parents' home and he confessed that over the past several months, he had become a regular user of methamphetamine, cocaine, marijuana, ecstasy, and heroin.

According to law enforcement officials, there is a good possibility that the group will be charged with a "conspiracy," and they are currently facing life imprisonment.

Sad, isn't it? Another young life shattered because of drugs. Another family shaking their heads and wondering what went wrong. And another reason why the drug epidemic must be curtailed.

Did you know that according to some research that forty-nine percent of teens admit to having smoked marijuana by age thirteen or younger?

Did you know that two out of five middle school students know a friend or classmate who has used acid, cocaine, or heroin?

Did you know that seventy-eight percent of high school students say that drugs are used, kept, and sold at their school?

The most recent estimate of cost to U.S. society of alcohol and other drug abuse was 246 billion dollars: 148 billion from alcohol abuse and 98 billion from other drug abuse.

I hope that you will recommit to making a difference to the students that we serve by taking a tough, new, aggressive stand in this war on drugs. As Randy sits in a jail cell awaiting trial, I'm sure that he wishes someone had helped steer him down a different path.

You see, I've known this promising young man most of his life...and while I am deeply saddened by this tragic turn of events, I am at the same time fueled with a renewed vigor that we must continue to fight for what is just and good for our children. We must never lose hope! We must never see ourselves as defeated in this "war."

For as Dale Carnegie once said: "Most of the important things in the world have been accomplished by people who have kept on trying when there seemed to be no hope at all."

Way back in 1970, Time Magazine ran an article about kids and the increasing dependency on illegal drugs. They referred to the phenomenon as an "adolescent epidemic."

Today's drug epidemic among our young is as real as cancer, as contagious as influenza, and as damaging as an accident between a motorcycle and an 18-wheeler.

And, in the meantime, we continue to utter each time we lose a child to this epidemic: "Oh, what might have been?"

"God's up there behind the blue.
Don't believe me? Watch this!
'Hey, God, stick your head out!'"

-- Grandson Luke, age 5,
explaining to his sister
that God was up above in Heaven.

CHAPTER FOUR

"Just When You Wonder if Anyone is Listening"

"Don't worry that children never listen to you; worry that they are always watching you."

Robert Fulghum

"Just When You Wonder if Anyone is Listening"

It started out like any other morning. I sat down at my desk, reached down and turned on the computer, then turned on my desk lamp.

While the computer went through its startup process, I discarded a few papers on my desk, glanced outside at the daffodils that had started blooming in the front flower bed, and although the skies were overcast, it looked like a pretty good day.

I heard the familiar chime of the computer, telling me that things were ready.

One click on a yellow icon launched Microsoft Office Outlook, and almost immediately the messages started stacking up.

"Seen that one." Delete. "Junk mail." Delete

"H-m-m-m-m. That name sounds vaguely familiar. Maybe I should open this one."

"Good morning, Mr. Jordan. You probably don't

remember me, but ..."

And for the next several minutes I read in rapt disbelief the words from a teacher I had met years ago.

Slowly, I began to recall the scene. West Texas. Teacher training. Visited briefly with a teacher and her teenage son. No dad in his life. Corresponded with them for a while.

That had been seven or eight years prior, and now the teacher was reminding me of that day. I had spoken to a group of teachers on a Saturday morning at a workshop in West Texas. The session, offered by the Education Service Center, had good attendance. One teacher had brought her 14-year old son, Steven.

Prior to the meeting, she had introduced me to him. During my presentation, I referenced him a couple of times, indicating how good it was to have him in attendance.

Now, as I read her e-mail, the memory of that morning came flooding back.

"My son and I had the pleasure of listening to you speak at a conference a few years ago. I believe that he was about 14 at the time. He is now 22. He and I e-mailed you for awhile and he kept one of the books you signed for him until our house burned and we lost everything.

"Steven is having a very difficult life. He is ill and may

have to have chemo. We won't know until later this month.

"You may recall that he had a very difficult school life, but in spite of it, he graduated.

"He lost his wife last May. He had some problems following her death, but he is coming out of it. He now works for the local newspaper and is doing better.

"After all these years, he has never forgotten you and the kindness that you showed to him. He talks about that conference from time to time. You really got him to listen to you and enjoy it.

"If you ever have some extra time, would you mind dropping Steven a line?"

For several moments I sat in stunned silence. Goodness gracious. It was such a small thing to share a few kind words with this young man, yet it had meant so much.

I wonder how often we touch a life and don't even realize it? I wonder how many times I've missed that opportunity because something else seemed far more important at the time. I wonder…

That e-mail had caused me to realize just how much some children are hurting. It had caused me to realize just how important it is for us to take the time to hear them, listen to them, and encourage them.

And in order to ensure that I didn't miss this

opportunity, I clicked on "Actions" at the top of the screen, and then scrolled down to "New Mail Message."

"Dear Steven...We met years ago at a conference that you attended with you mom. Gosh, how the years fly by. I've never forgotten you, Steven, and just wanted to catch up ...

CHAPTER FIVE

"If Only We Were *in loco parentis*"

"You don't really understand human nature unless you know why a child on a merry-go-round will wave at his parents every time around - and why his parents will always wave back."

-- William D. Tammeus

If Only We Lovingly Were
"In Loco Parentis"

Do you ever get the feeling that everyone you meet these days is an expert on all issues?

It doesn't matter if it is politics, or religion, or education, it seems that there are more people than ever who are challenging what we do in public education.

As I talk to teachers and administrators, it seems that more and more of the pressure is coming from parents and guardians who tell the professional educator how they should teach, how they should run the schools, how they should treat their children.

"The parents are driving me crazy," one teacher told me recently. "I get a note from some of them every single day, and they're complaining about something I said, or did, or didn't do. It seems that I'm spending more time training the parents than I am teaching their children."

What has happened? What has caused this sudden explosion of excessive parental harassment? Why are educators suddenly the "bad guys?"

Well, for one thing, far too many educators have lost

the respect and dignity that they once had.

Oh, I know. We don't like to hear this... but it is the truth.

When we pick up the newspaper or turn on the television almost any day of the week we learn of some teacher who has violated a child. It sends a frightening message and alerts us as parents that we need to be certain that our children are safe and secure.

Forgive me for so many references to the way "things used to be," but teaching was at one time a most revered profession. Teachers dressed as professionals. They were exemplary role models in the community. They were truly "in loco parentis."

In case you've forgotten this remarkable and applicable Latin term, it means "in the place of the parent," or "instead of a parent." What a testament to the respect and admiration of an educator! We have been given, by law, authority and responsibility to act in the best interest of the student, just as a parent would do.

Unfortunately, some in our profession have forgotten what this "oath," almost sacred in nature, implies. Think about it! We are to serve and provide and love and care for the students as if *we* were the parent!

Becoming a parent years ago changed my entire life. I never realized how much you could love children until we had three of our own. That love was, quite simply, insurmountable! The very idea of anyone or anything harming one of my children was a horrifying thought.

I wrote an article years ago about how important and critical it is for educators to genuinely care about children. I even went so far as to say that I thought it was the single-most important "ingredient" for a teacher to possess.

A teacher, who was given a copy of the article by her principal, wrote me a scathing letter about how foolish I was. She stated something to the effect that she did *not* love her students. That was not why she was hired, and that her task was to teach them mathematics *...nothing else!*

Immediately upon reading that letter, my heart ached for both her *and* her students. From her remarks, I realized that she was not happy in her job and I strongly suspected that her students were just as miserable in her classroom.

Today, just for a moment, ponder on the idea that you are the parent of a very, very large family. Focus on the idea that you want the very best for "your children." Imagine what your school or your classroom would look like if it really did love the children enough to provide what was best for *each* child.

Would some of the teachers remain on your staff? Would courses be added which would strengthen and encourage special gifts a child has been given? Would you really want your child in a classroom where academics were more important than acceptance?

If you truly cared as much as a loving parent, would things remain the same?

I wonder. I really do wonder.

CHAPTER SIX

"And Then the Coach had an Unusual Idea..."

"People look at me and see a calm, cool guy on the sidelines and I want them to know that my Christian faith affects my coaching and everything I do."

--Tony Dungy

"And Then the Coach Had an Unusual Idea..."

The retired teacher didn't recognize the name on the return address as she slowly opened up the envelope.

"I just wanted to say 'thank you' for all you did for me back when I was in your seventh grade classroom. I've never forgotten the extra time you gave me. You took the time to listen to me when it seemed that no one else would. My husband and I have three children, and when I remind them to show their manners and be kind to others, I think of you."

Yes, getting a 'thank you' is one of the great rewards of our profession. Let's face it, ours can often be a thankless job and we need to treasure those times when others recognize our efforts with a sincere and heartfelt "thank you.'

Oh, I guess "thank you's" can be overdone. I'm reminded of the 15-year-old who once told his parents that whenever he was reading a good book, he would stop and thank his teacher. "That is," he added, "until she got an unlisted number."

But occasionally, you hear of something done by a teacher that is truly extraordinary.

Such is the case of Coach Kris Hogan. Because he currently works for a private school, his football schedule is a bit different from most public high schools.

This particular season he was slated to play the Gainesville, Texas Tornadoes in a Friday night football game. You may not have heard of the Tornadoes, but, at that time, they were a team of about thirteen young boys who have made a mistake or two, and ended up in the Gainesville State School for Boys. This school is operated by the Texas Youth Commission and is a fenced, maximum-security facility.

Coach Hogan started studying his opponent, and was suddenly struck with the realization that they couldn't have much of a fan base. All of their games were played on the opponent's fields, and the only ones who followed them week after week were a handful of staff members who worked at the state school. After all, most of these kids had come from dysfunctional and broken homes, so it was rare for a family member to be at the game to support them.

Because Coach Hogan realized that all kids needed to know someone cares about them, he developed a plan to encourage his fans to sit on the visitor's side of the stadium and cheer for the opponents on this special night. Knowing that this was a bit unorthodox, he told his parents that he wanted to let the team from Gainesville know that someone cared about them.

That night, hundreds showed up and filled both the

home and visitor's sides of the stadium. As the Tornadoes came out of the locker room, they couldn't believe their eyes, or their ears. A long "spirit line" had been formed. Many were wearing the Tornadoes school colors. Up ahead was a giant banner that had been made for them to run through. These fans erupted into ear-shattering cheers as they burst through the large Tornado banner and came crashing onto the field. This was truly unlike anything these guys had ever experienced.

When the game ended, no one really cared who had won or lost. When scores of locals rushed onto the field to congratulate them, tears welled-up in the player's eyes as they were embraced by the new fans.

Can't you just feel the emotion as you visualize this event. Total strangers are embracing these kids. They are congratulating them. They're slapping them on the back and taking their pictures.

As one on the Tornadoes team said, "I couldn't believe there was actually someone in our corner. I'm not embarrassed to say that when I got back in the locker room, I cried like a baby. I've never known so many people cared how I felt."

So for one star-filled Texas Friday night, thirteen young men who assumed they had been forgotten by the world, kept shaking their heads and saying, "Oh, my goodness! That was amazing! Thank you!"

And I, for one, have no doubt they meant it.

AUTHOR'S NOTE: A special "thank you" to Coach Kris Hogan and the students and staff of Faith Christian School in Grapevine, Texas for realizing that winning a kid is far more important than winning a game.

CHAPTER SEVEN

"No Music? No Art? What a Dull World This Would Be"

"Art is the signature of civilization."

--Beverly Sills

"No music? No art? What a dull world this would be!"

Could I just put in a plug for the arts?

Oh, I know we all think that fine arts in our public schools is important, but there just isn't enough money to go around for all of these "extras," is there?

Do you mind if I just share a couple of statistics with you? Did you know that in a 1997 UCLA study it was discovered that students who had a "high involvement" in the arts consistently made better scores on standardized tests than those who had little or no exposure to the arts?

In July, 2004, Ron Page, then Secretary of Education, wrote a letter to superintendents all over the country regarding the arts "as a core academic subject" and a vital part of the *No Child Left Behind* act.

He stated: "I believe the arts have a significant role in education both for their intrinsic value and for the ways in which they can enhance general academic achievement and improve students' social and emotional environment."

He went on to say that "the arts, perhaps more than

any other subject, help students to understand themselves and others..."

My, my! So, if it was included in the *No Child Left Behind* act, why are the arts taking such a backseat to other "core academic subjects?"

Perhaps it is because we don't "test" the arts. There is nothing on state-wide testing about art, or music, or drama or dance. We only test what some refer to as the "major" academic areas.

And, as a result, we spend more and more time on math, language arts, writing, and other "major" subject areas.

How sad.

As David Woods from the University of Connecticut wrote, most school districts focus "on those subject areas that will be assessed and tested and disregard the fact that literacy goes beyond reading and writing and encompasses the more global perspective of how we make meaning in our world."

Wow!

Oh, and I've heard the argument that some folks make: "That's the parent's responsibility."

Well, to those I say: "Maybe athletics ought to be the parents' responsibility. Or maybe writing should be left up to Mom and Dad. And what about foreign language?"

Oh, the list really is endless!

In my opinion, for what it's worth, if we would truly capitalize on each student's individual gifts and provide worthwhile curriculum to meet those gifts, we would see a great many more students stay in school and graduate with a truly worthwhile sack of knowledge.

It's just a suggestion.

Some once said, "I believe education in music, theater, dance, and the visual arts is one of the most creative ways we have to find the gold that is buried just underneath the surface."

Gosh I wish I had said that. Because I believe it with all my heart!

Recently, my wife and I attended a concert by the Fort Worth Symphony at the extraordinary Bass Hall in Fort Worth, Texas. As I waited for the program to begin, I suddenly realized that there were no children present.

I leaned over the rail, surveying row upon row beneath me, and could not see one single child!

During the entire performance, I couldn't get it out of my mind. Here we were, listening to some of the most beautiful music I had ever heard, and there were no young ears to absorb it. There were no aspiring musicians to be inspired by it. There were no small children to marvel at the music coming from the wide array of instruments.

Perhaps if young children had been made aware of great music in our schools, they would have longed to have been present.

You and I both know that every one of our students has been blessed with a gift. For some it is, indeed, academics. For others, it is athletics. For others, it is one of the fine arts.

If "no child is to be left behind," I believe we are truly leaving the gifted arts student "behind" if, as a public school, we do not make every effort to help develop his or her God-given gift and offer the arts as intensely as we do the other offerings.

Maybe you've seen these two quotes by Pablo Picasso. I think they make my point crystal clear.

"Every child is an artist; the problem is how to remain an artist once he grows up."

And Picasso also said: My mother said to me, 'If you become a soldier, you'll be a general; if you become a monk, you'll end up as the pope.' Instead, I became a painter and wound up as Picasso."

I rest my case.

CHAPTER EIGHT

"Teaching Them to Make Good Choices"

"It's not hard to make decisions
when you know what your values are."

-- Roy Disney

Teaching Them
to Make Good Choices:
One of Our Greatest Challenges

Peer pressure is really an unbelievably strong force, isn't it?

Oh, I'm sure that you see it every day. A student does something totally out of character. Generally, it is because of peer pressure. A teacher may react differently than her conscience tells her. It is often peer pressure from another adult.

I read once of a study conducted several years ago by psychologist Ruth Berenda and her associates. They wanted to see just how powerful peer pressure was among various age groups.

Their plan was quite simple. They selected a group of ten individuals of approximately the same age and brought them into a room together. They were told that they were going to be shown three separate charts and once the teacher pointed to the one they believed had the longest line on it, they were to raise their hand.

However, unbeknownst to one member of the group was the fact that the other nine had been told to select the second-longest line each time.

Their aim was to determine how a single individual would react when surrounded by a large group who voted just the opposite of what the individual knew to be the "right" way to respond.

Well, you guessed it. The "guinea pig" went along with the "crowd" every time. Oh, at first he was quick to vote the way he thought was really right, but when everyone else voted just the opposite, researchers began to see a look of doubt on his face, and after a time or two, he voted with the group.

Why? I'm sure it was for the same reason that each of us, at one time or another, has wanted to go another route, but we didn't want to face the stares of our colleagues. We didn't want to chance having someone make a remark that might hurt us. We didn't want to be excluded.

And, can you imagine the pressure on our students each day? They are faced with decisions which will either make them "accepted" or "rejected" by their peers. The decisions they make will either get them praise from their peers or remarks which tear at the very soul. What an unpleasant position in which to be.

Comedian Steven Wright once said, "Hermits have no peer pressure."

He meant it to be funny, and there is an element of it that is humorous. However, when talking about our students, the last thing we want them to become is a hermit. We want them to be active, to be involved, and to live life to its fullest.

I remember a friend of mine when I was in high school. What a great guy. Everyone loved his wit, his smile, and his friendship. He was so bright. His future looked so promising.

Yet, in spite of everything he had going for him, he could not resist a dare. When challenged, it was almost as if he felt he had to do something ridiculous in order to be accepted. He started drinking on a dare from some classmates, and the next thing you knew, he was drinking regularly. After graduation, he couldn't seem to keep a job because of his drinking problem, and before long he was drafted and sent to Viet Nam. His letters began to reveal an even more troubling side when he began to almost brag about using drugs that were readily available.

A few years later, he came home, and those of us who had known him prior to the war could hardly believe our eyes. The conservative haircut had been traded for long, unkempt hair; the smile had been traded for a sneer; and the wit had been traded for sarcasm and bitterness.

It was so obvious that he was more unhappy with himself than with anyone else. He couldn't keep a job. He was angry. He was spiraling out of control. He knew it. We all knew it.

Some of us talked with him for hours on end about getting help, but our pleas apparently came too late.

Some six months after returning home, authorities found his body slumped against a tree. A pistol with one spent cartridge lay beside him.

I'll never forget him, and will always wonder how differently things might have been if he had been able to withstand the pressure from those around him… *and* from the "demons" within him.

In my opinion, teaching our students to make good choices is one of the greatest lessons that they can learn. Let's teach them courage, how to stand up for what is right, and when to say "no."

What Thomas Paine wrote in 1776 to encourage the patriots is just as applicable today for those of us who want to make the world a better place for future generations:

"The harder the conflict, the more glorious the triumph. What we obtain too cheap, we esteem too lightly; it is dearness only that gives everything its value. I love the man that can smile in trouble, that can gather strength from distress and grow brave by reflection. 'Tis the business of little minds to shrink; but he whose heart is firm, and whose conscience approves his conduct, will pursue his principles unto death."

And I believe that deserves a big "Amen."

CHAPTER NINE

"Today a Weed ...
Tomorrow a Hybrid"

"Instruction does much... but encouragement everything."

-- Johann Wolfgang von Goethe

"Today a Weed ...
Tomorrow a Hybrid"

It was a perfectly perfect spring day. The wind had stopped its March madness and only a cool gentle breeze blew across the Texas landscape. The wildflowers were at their peak, as bluebonnets, wine cups, and a host of unidentified flora sauntered back and forth across a field of more green than you would find on St. Patrick's Day.

It was captivating. It was euphoric. It was better than any tranquilizer on the market. And then, amongst all of this natural beauty, I spied a plant that towered above the rest. Its leaves were spiked from one end to the other. Small, sharp nettles protruded from every stem and stalk. Its leaves weren't green, but gray. They had a slight silver luster to them.

"Yuk," I said almost instinctively. "Wish I had my garden hoe with me. I'd chop that prickly thing down in a minute."

"Really now," responded the gentlemen walking alongside me. "You might want to find out a bit more about that 'ugly duckling' before you chop her down."

"Why would I want to do that?" I asked with a puzzled look on my face.

"Because if you look long enough and hard enough, you might discover that there's beauty there that's waiting to bloom."

"OK," I said. "I'll give it a chance."

Well, I don't know about you, but unless I act right then and there, I tend to forget about such matters after only a few minutes. And such was this case. I didn't do any research. I didn't go back and study the plant. I just ignored it.

Several weeks later, I'm once again strolling through this wildflower haven, when something across the way caught my eye. Suddenly, I was a man on a mission. With my eyes focused straight ahead, I walked as if I was in a trance. For there, in the middle of this field of withering bluebonnets, grew a plant that was covered in the most delicate white flowers I had ever seen.

"Why, they're beautiful," I muttered as butterflies danced from flower to flower on the spiked plant. Words could not begin to describe the almost transparent petals that surrounded a soft yellow center. Yes, this plant was breathtaking.

I would later learn that this plant is a white prickly poppy, limited somewhat to the southwest. In addition to the beautiful flowers it produces, its seeds are an excellent source of food for many varieties of birds. Surprisingly, the oil from this plant was used as an alternative lubricant during World War II.

And then I remembered the words my friend had spoken a few weeks earlier: *"If you look long enough and hard enough, you might discover that there's beauty there that's waiting to bloom."*

As I stood there looking at this plant that I had almost discarded, I couldn't help but think of how often kids get the same "quick-to-judge" treatment.

They don't look or dress like the "pretty" kids, so they're written off rather quickly. "That one's got to be a weed," we're told.

For whatever reason, they're not able to achieve academically as well as some of the others. "Ought to put that one in a special class," someone quickly suggests.

They tend to look for attention in all the wrong ways. "No good can come from that one," another mutters.

But then, we remember that every kid has a gift that is just waiting to be discovered, not discarded; encouraged, not eliminated; developed, not destroyed.

And just like the prickly plant that stands back and waits to bloom, every child has the potential to blossom one day, and often does it with only a small amount of encouragement.

There are so many stories about children who achieved success in spite of over-whelming obstacles. Did you ever hear the story of the young boy who loved to write – in spite of the fact that he had attended school only four years of his young life? At a young age, he found himself on the streets, sleeping in abandoned buildings and finally, out of necessity, he took a job in a rat-infested warehouse gluing labels onto bottles.

But this kid, with all the appearances of a "thistle," loved to write. And time and time again his stories were rejected by publishers.

But it only took one acceptance, one word of encouragement, for this young man to write more than ever.

Perhaps you've heard of him. His name is quite legendary. The young boy who appeared to have no future was Charles Dickens, author of *David Copperfield, A Christmas Carol,* and so many other great works of literature.

Do you have such a gifted student somewhere in your life? That single word of encouragement might be all it takes for that child to blossom into a hybrid.

Remember: *"If you look long enough and hard enough, you might discover that there's beauty there that's waiting to bloom."*

CHAPTER TEN

"The Best Evaluation Ever"

"Everything that can be counted does not necessarily count; everything that counts cannot necessarily be counted"

-- Albert Einstein

"The Best Evaluation Ever"

Once upon a time there was a teacher who was assigned to a new school because of increased enrollment. She was the new kid on the block. She would have to do her best to find extra teachers' editions of the textbooks. She would have to beg for enough desks to provide one for each student. She was the one on the team who would have few supplies because this was a new section, and there just weren't enough to go around.

Her excitement of teaching these young elementary students was overwhelming. She spent weeks preparing her room prior to the first day of classes. She used what little money she had to buy new books and materials. These would be used in centers and displays around the room.

"It needs to be bright and inviting," she told herself.

The other teachers on her team seemed nice enough, although they were busy preparing their own rooms, and didn't have enough time to help the new teacher.

On the first day of school, she was there early. She wanted everything to be perfect for these youngsters to whom she was entrusted for an entire year of their lives.

The first one or two were a bit over-active, but she knew that most of them would be well-behaved and ready to learn.

One by one they arrived, each seemingly more active than the previous one. By 8:01, they were all in the room, but few of them were in their seats.

It didn't take long to realize that this was either an exceptionally rowdy group, or she had been given a selected list of students that the other teachers didn't particularly want in their own rooms.

As the students began to take their seats, she realized that the desks had not been raised to accommodate her grade-level of students. The room had been a lower grade classroom the previous year, so the desks had not been adjusted.

During her lunch time, she raised twenty-two desks one notch higher in order to make the desks more comfortable for her students. With nothing but a screw driver, she adjusted the eighty-eight legs.

"The rest of the day was just a disaster," she said. "I felt like a complete failure."

But as the students began to leave, they smiled, said their "good-byes," and rushed to the bus for the ride home.

One young boy, however, stayed behind. In her mind, he had received the distinction of being the most active child in the room. He had talked incessantly. He had rarely sat in his seat. He had not been able to stay focused.

With a grin from ear to ear, he came up to her, and with eyes sparkling, he said, "I don't want to go home. This has been the best day ever!"

She wanted to hug him, to laugh, to cry. A flood of emotions ran through her simultaneously.

Finally, she swallowed and managed to say, "Why, thank you, Charlie. You just made my day!" And, indeed he had.

For those in education, the rewards may come slowly, but they will come.

And when they do, it makes us realize the real reason we became educators.

So now that school has been underway for a few weeks, take a moment to re-evaluate your reasons for working with children.

The checklist might look something like this:

☑ Has establishing a relationship with the students been my main objective?
☑ Do my students know that I'm always ready to listen?
☑ Have I been a good role model for them in the way I have responded to problems?

☑ Have I encouraged them on a regular basis?
☑ Have I been patient with those who need it the most?
☑ Do I reflect that I'm glad to see them each day?
☑ Have I discovered anything about their life at home?
☑ Do they know I truly care about them by my actions?

Your evaluation doesn't always come from a school administrator. The most accurate one comes from the child who says, "I don't want to go home. This has been the best day ever!"

CHAPTER ELEVEN

"A Tribute to a Special Lady"

"My mother was the most beautiful woman I ever saw. All I am I owe to my mother. I attribute all my success in life to the moral, intellectual and physical education I received from her."

-- George Washington

"A Tribute to a Special Lady"

She was one of six children and moved constantly.

"I can't remember all the houses we lived in," she would say, "but Momma always kept it clean and orderly."

Because neither her mother nor father had a formal schooling, education was not considered a priority in her family.

At an early age, she picked cotton during the season. They simply moved from town to town to work in the fields, and what little money she made went into the family pot to cover the necessary items in life. There was none left for the latest clothing styles or books or toys or games or bicycles.

Oh, she did get to go to school a few months out of the year. She generally got to enroll in the closest public school in late November or early December, but then the corn and bean fields began calling, so in early spring, she would be gone again.

She once recalled that it was a teacher who employed her one entire summer.

"It was one of the best times in my life," she would tell folks. "She even made me a new dress, the first one I'd ever had."

The teacher taught her how to iron and make beds and set a table. But more than anything else, she taught her to always be positive.

"She was one of the nicest people I ever met," she reminded herself.

She quit going to school in the fifth grade, because as she said, "I was too big for the desks and the kids would laugh at me."

She married the first time at the age of sixteen. A baby quickly followed, but the working in the fields continued.

"When I got married, I went with his family wherever there was work. I'd pick cotton for fourteen hours a day, and I was good at it. I could out pick any man!" she would say proudly.

The living quarters were now tents that were set up at one end of the field. The dirt floors were swept. The meals were cooked on a campfire. And the money she made was handed over to the mother-in-law.

"I never got to keep a penny of it," she added.

For whatever reason from the long list, the marriage ended soon after the baby was born.

Now it was back with her parents, living in a wooden shack with no electricity, no indoor plumbing, and a roof that leaked.

But her stay with her parents was not to last long, because she met a man twenty-plus years older than she was, and fell madly in love. They married, had a baby boy and a baby girl and lived happily together for thirty-nine years.

"Oh, they weren't always easy, but Arthur and I managed. He started out being a rancher, but times got hard, so he did anything he could to support our family. And when things got really rough, he went to work driving a garbage truck. He'd bring home lots of good things that people threw away. We clothed our kids with a lot of it."

Those who knew her often recalled her words of wisdom: "There's no excuse for being dirty. Soap and water are cheap!"

"Whatever you do, make it your best."

"Don't knock somethin' until you've tried it."

"You be sure you get an education…and get a good one!"

"Remember, if you get a whippin' at school, you're gonna get one when you get home!"

"You can do anything you set your mind to."

Her husband died shortly after her fifty-ninth birthday.

"It's awful hard to give up those you love," she said as tears began filling her eyes.

In spite of her up-bringing, she was always cheerful, and loving, and there to help those who needed it. She went to night school in her sixties and earned a GED.

"I just wanted something to show that I wasn't ignorant," she said. "I knew I could do it."

Quite frankly, she was one of the smartest and kindest people I've ever known.

This wise, good-natured, beautiful woman was my mother…and she passed away in 2008 at the age of eighty-seven. My sister and I are the two children of Lillian and Arthur.

And just like she said when Daddy died in 1980, I found myself saying over and over, "It's awful hard to give up those you love."

Rest in peace, Momma.

CHAPTER TWELVE

"Thanking a Teacher ...
It's Long Overdue!"

"I have come to believe that a great teacher is a great artist and that there are as few as there are any other great artists. Teaching might even be the greatest of the arts since the medium is the human mind and spirit."

-- John Steinbeck

Thanking a Teacher.
It's Long Overdue!

Someone recently sent me a list of things that adults see one way... and kids see another.

For example, when we see a puddle of muddy water, we avoid it. We see it as something to mess up our shoes, track into the house, and definitely something to avoid.

When a child sees it, however, he sees it as a place to splash in, make imaginary rivers, float sticks, and have a wonderful time.

Oh, to be a child again.

Well, the article got me to thinking about how the world sees things... as opposed to how teachers and others educators view them.

When the world sees low test scores, they see a school that needs to work harder. When educators see low test scores, they see it as challenge and realize once again that this year's class is not the same as last year's.

When the world sees a tax increase, they see it as extravagant and not needed. When educators see a tax increase, they see needs being met that had to be "band-aided" before.

When the world hears of a teacher who had to leave the classroom because she couldn't handle it, they see it as one who couldn't take the heat. When school employees see such a teacher, their heart breaks because they know she cared too much.

When the world sees an individual commit a horrendous act against society, they cry out that the school should have seen it coming. When the school hears about the former student, they remember a family and a society that failed him long before he enrolled in school.

When the world discovers a new problem, such as AIDS, or a drug epidemic, they turn to the school and say, "Solve it." When the school learns of the problem, they silently think, "How can I possibly include one more thing? ... But it needs to be done."

When the world sees a family of hungry children, they look the other way. When a teacher sees a hungry child, she feeds him, knowing that a hungry child could never learn.

When the world reads of the death of a mother or father, they say, "How sad." When the teacher reads of the loss of a mother or father, they put their arms around the child and comfort him as he silently weeps.

When the world complains that the schools are too easy on kids these days because there's no corporal punishment, the teacher simply says that there are better ways to improve a child than with more pain in his or her life.

When the world screams that our kids aren't getting as good of an education as they are in foreign countries, the teacher smiles and says, "Have you noticed how many of those youngsters from around the world are attending our colleges and universities?"

However, when the world says that schools aren't providing enough opportunities for kids, such as vocational or art or music or drama, the teacher quietly says, "I agree with you."

When the world says there are too many kids in a classroom, the teacher nods her head and says, "I didn't think you had noticed."

When the world says that the schools are not safe enough for kids today, the teacher says, "You're right. We could use your help."

But when the world reports that their children have finished their education, and have a good job, and are model citizens, the teacher says, "Yes. I recognized that quality in your child years ago."

Thank you, teachers, for your genuine love for children, for your compassion, for your understanding, for your desire to improve a life, for your gentleness, and for sharing your amazing gift.

For although we may not tell you very often, you

continue to make an incredible difference in the lives of our children.

And thanking you is *long* overdue!

CHAPTER THIRTEEN

"Bird Houses
and Embroider Hoops!
Yikes! It's "Cousin's Camp!"

"My new exercise is chasing my grandchildren."

--Author Unknown

Bird Houses
and Embroider Hoops!
Yikes! It's "Cousin's Camp!"

It's funny how just a phrase or short sentence spoken by the right person at the right time can change your life.

A friend of ours was talking a few years ago and she mentioned that she was getting ready for "Cousin's Camp." You see, she would invite the grandchildren to come together and get to know each other better in a week-long visit she called "Cousin's Camp."

It sounded like such a great idea. So, my wife Karen and I began formulating this plan to do a camp for the grandkids.

At that time, we had seven grandchildren, but we only invited five. The two smallest ones, ages one and two, would have to come to us a little later. I told the wife that I was sure that there was some state regulation prohibiting us from having seven children, ages one to fourteen, in our home for a week.

The invitations were extended and preparations were begun.

Almost immediately, I told Karen that we needed to develop a "strategic plan," a "mission statement," a "vision statement," and even asked if we needed to bring in a consultant.

Hey, don't tell me that all of that training as a school administrator didn't come in handy!

She looked at me with *that* look and rolled her eyes. I figured that she had given me all the feedback I needed, so I hushed.

"Well, if we're not going to do all of that," I finally said, "I'll plan activities for the three boys and you plan something for the two girls."

I know. There are government regulations prohibiting these kind of "sexist" plans, but I was determined that I could get by with it for a week before the feds moved in.

It was agreed that the boys could build bird houses and that the girls would learn to embroider.

A trip to the lumber yard for cedar boards, drills, nails, wood glue, sandpaper, etc. cost as much as our first house payment. Karen came out a little better with her purchase of fabric, iron-on designs, thread, needles, hoops, etc.

Prior to their arrival, I cut out all of the pieces for each bird house. I soon realized that I had incorrectly figured the amount of wood I needed, and had enough for each of the guys to have *two* birdhouses.

"Good plan," I thought. "When that first one is finished, I'll surprise them with a second one."

When they finally arrived at our home on that hot, summer afternoon, you could feel the excitement in the air. While they were dragging in their luggage, I began to announce: "Cousin's Camp conference! Cousin's Camp conference! Five minutes. Report to the back yard."

Oh, they were loving this.

Once assembled, we told them about the plan for the boys to build birdhouses and the girls to do embroidered cup towels.

"We want to do birdhouses, too!" the girls exclaimed. "That's not fair."

"It's too hot to be outside doing birdhouses," the boys said. "Let's do something inside."

So, that's when all of our plans changed.

During the day, we *all* worked on our birdhouses under a big pecan tree in the backyard. In the evening, while sitting in air-conditioned comfort, we *all* did embroidery.

No television. No loud music. No distractions. It was wonderful.

It also had to be some scenes I shall never forget. I wished for Norman Rockwell.

Those petite little girls hammering and sanding and building was just priceless. And then those three boys, with needle in hand and hoop in lap, scattered over the den and working diligently to do their best will forever be etched into my mind.

The week flew by. We swam a couple of days. We took in one movie. We cooked out. We had the finals for the World Championship Pogo Tournament. By the end of the week there had been no accidents, no sick children, no major disagreements.

Oh, what was supposed to have been six identical looking birdhouses turned out to be six diversely different looking birdhouses. And, the embroidered cup towels probably won't win an award at the state fair, but oh, they are beautiful!

We all cried and hugged when it was time for all the grandkids to leave. Cousin's Camp had been a tremendous success ... even without strategic plan.

And just before they piled into their cars, the winner of the pogo championship decided to show his parents how well he had learned to jump down our stone steps on the pogo stick. You guessed it. He fell ... and a trip to the emergency room showed that he would need to be in a special boot for several weeks while his ankle healed.

Once they were back from the emergency room and all strapped in for the trip back home, there he was, with his foot propped up, wearing a boot that looked twice his size, sitting in the back seat with an embroidery hoop, needle and thread.

We are already planning for next year's event.

"Two of the greatest gifts I was ever given are my unusual name ... and a hairpiece.

It's hard to get too high and mighty with a name like 'Riney' and a hairpiece that could blow off at any minute."

-- Riney Jordan

CHAPTER
FOURTEEN

"Oh, the Joy and Wisdom of Grandchildren"

"What a bargain grandchildren are!
I give them my loose change and they give
me a million dollars worth of pleasure!

-- Gene Perrett

Oh, the Joy and Wisdom of Grandchildren

There they were. Two precious children playing in the sandbox while Mom & Dad worked in the yard, but these parents were ever mindful of the actions of those two little gifts from God.

It was a beautiful summer day, with a deep, rich blue sky overhead.

As the mother and father pulled weeds and trimmed shrubs, they quietly listened as the 3-year old shared his earthly wisdom with his two-year old sister.

The discussion began with comments about the proper construction of a sand castle. Then the attention focused on an insect crawling across the sand. They sang together for a while.

Suddenly Luke said to Anna: "God lives up there behind the blue."

"Where?" she asked.

"Up there… behind the blue," Luke responded with all the confidence a three-year old could muster.

"Where?" she asked again. "I don't see God."

"He's up there *behind* the blue," Luke said again. "You can't see Him because He's BEHIND the blue!"

The Mom and Dad couldn't help but look at each other and smile. Oh, it was good to listen to the wisdom, the understanding, the simplicity of those two little children.

This was better than any other entertainment they could imagine.

Anna's face furrowed as she stared heavenward. Her eyes squinted as she strained to see exactly where this God was "behind the blue."

"I still don't see Him," she said matter-of-factly.

"OK," Luke said. "I'll show you!"

And with that he began yelling at the top of his little lungs: "GOD! G-o-o-o-o-d-d-d-d-d!"

This loud summons prompted Anna to join right in.

"G-O-O-O-O-O-O-O-D-D-D-D-D-D-D!" she yelled.

The Mom and Dad looked at each other as if to say, "U-h-h-h.... what do we do?"

And then the two children started taking turns yelling for God.

"God!" he screamed.

"God!" she echoed.

"God!" he yelled.

"God!" she resounded again.

And then, as if God needed a little coaxing, Luke stood up, looked skyward, put his little hands on his hips and yelled, "God! STICK...YOUR...HEAD...OUT!"

Oh, how I love to hear these stories about our grandchildren. My, my... they are precious!

When you are around children, I hope we will recognize the fact and remember that while youngsters don't have all the answers, they are naturally curious.

While they don't have all the resources, they are remarkably resourceful.

And while they are still innocent, they have am amazing trust in those who show they care.

They have a trust in us as parents, in us as teachers, in us as leaders in our schools. Let us ever be mindful of the awesome responsibility that we have to these children to whom we have been entrusted.

Stick your head out and look around.

Take your head out of the screams of our critics and hold it high.

Take your head out of the fog and refocus on those basics that we know in our hearts are good for children.

Take your head out of the policy manuals and look into the eyes of the children you serve.

Take yourself out of the offices and visit the classrooms.

Rediscover the joy of children. Rediscover the excitement of working in their lives. Rediscover the thrill that comes from making a difference in the lives of these youngsters who need us so badly.

For as someone once said, "A child reminds us that playtime is an essential part of our daily routine."

I encourage you to have the faith of a child today. Look up into the blue. Look all around you. Look into the eyes of children.

You might just be surprised where you find God.

CHAPTER FIFTEEN

"What did I ever do to make my Mom hate me?"

"It's easier to build up a child than it is to repair an adult. Choose your words wisely."

-- Author Unknown

"What did I ever do to make my Mom hate me?"

I'm often accused of writing too many sad and touching stories about kids, but get ready, because I've just heard about one that broke my heart. I know it will yours, too.

While visiting the local hardware store recently, I asked the lady clerk how her two grandsons were doing that she was raising. I had gotten to know them through my grandson, who often had them over for a visit.

"When I was first married, I wanted a child more than anything in the world. I would have done almost anything to have a baby. An adoption agency offered me a beautiful little baby girl and I quickly agreed to adopt her. However, it wasn't too many years before I realized that she had some serious emotional problems. Medical doctors, psychiatrists and other specialists tried everything to discuss why she had such fits of rage.

By now, I was drawn into her story and felt such sadness for her.

She then began relating how her adopted daughter started running with the wrong crowd once she became a teenager. Before long she discovered she was pregnant. She had the baby and almost immediately started staying out late, coming home intoxicated, and, like so many, got involved in drugs. Another baby followed, and she announced that she was not going to stay home and miss out on her "good time."

"You raise 'em," she told her mother.

"So, I've had them ever since," she said with a blank stare. "I love those two little boys and now, they call me 'Mom.'"

As she continued, I learned that the mother's whereabouts were usually not known.

"When she's in jail somewhere is about the only time we know where she is," she said.

"But this past weekend, something happened that I will never allow to happen again."

A look of firm determination had crossed her face and I knew that she was going to feel strongly about what followed.

It seems that the boy's birth mom had called and wanted to talk to the younger one.

"He was smiling and beaming from ear to ear when he hung up the phone. His mom had told him that she would be by on Saturday to pick him up and take him to a movie, or wherever he wanted to go. She would do the same thing later for the older one. She wanted to spend some time with her boys.

"He was ecstatic!" she related.

On Saturday morning, the six-year-old was up early, dressed, combed his hair and waited anxiously for mom to arrive.

I know you know what happened next – or should I say, "didn't" happen?

He sat there, looking out the window occasionally, and around noon, realized that she wasn't going to be there.

"He cried the rest of the day," the loving grandmother replied.

Tears came to her eyes as she told the story.

"He came over at one point, crawled up into my lap, and said, 'What did I ever do to make my mom hate me so much?"

Like most children, he assumed it was his fault. He took the blame for his circumstances.

"I assured him that it wasn't anything he had done, and then I held him for the longest time," she said.

With tears suddenly rolling down both of our cheeks, I gave her a hug and spoke softly in her ear.

"Thank you for loving those boys and making such a

positive difference in their lives."

Oh, my … what some parents do to children! It's almost unthinkable, almost unbelievable, almost unimaginable, isn't it? Yet, as educators and parents, we *know* that it happens. Everyday, somewhere, children are being ignored, punished, hurt, neglected, abused, shamed. Oh, the list is endless.

And for that reason, if for no other, we have a responsibility, an obligation, to do everything in our power to see that the students we serve are loved, cared for, and made to feel secure.

State-wide testing may be important, but nothing is more important to a child's development than TIME.

More than ever, it's time to focus on the child. Commit to bringing some joy and comfort to those children who are hurting.

I promise that it will be one of the most productive actions you've ever taken as an educator.

CHAPTER SIXTEEN

"It's Time to Do Something About 'Grumpy'"

"I am determined to be cheerful and happy in whatever situation I may find myself. For I have learned that the greater part of our misery or unhappiness is determined not by our circumstance but by our disposition."

--Martha Washington

It's Time to Do Something About "Grumpy"

Is time really going by at the same speed as it did when I was younger? For example, something called "summer vacation" has been relegated to a few weeks between "staff development" and "family development," and far too often, the "family" gets the short end of the deal.

I once spoke to a large group of transportation administrators and bus drivers. Here are the folks who truly do set the tone for the students each morning.

Got a grumpy bus driver? You'll probably have that rub off on some kids.

On the other hand, if you have a driver who likes children, interacts with them, and brightens their morning, you'll unload a group of youngsters who, in all likelihood, will have a good start that day.

One driver came up to me following the presentation and said in a hushed voice, "I'm so glad you talked about 'grumpy' bus drivers! I've got one that is so grumpy, the kids are afraid of him!"

No matter what your job in our public schools, vow right now to be upbeat, cheerful, and thankful every day. The children are our "customers," and they should be treated with the utmost respect and appreciation.

I know what you're saying, "Oh, sure! But if you knew the kids we've got in our district, in our school, you'd understand why that doesn't work!"

And, I can almost hear my momma saying, "But remember, two wrongs don't make a right!"

And, of course, she's right!

I recently visited in the home of some of the youngsters in our church's children's program. Here were six children, ranging in ages from ten to four. Two or three men had fathered these children, yet the one living there on this day wasn't the father of any of them. I flinched a bit, I'm sure, when he said, "…but we're hoping to have one of our own before long."

Several dogs and cats also occupied this place they called home. Most of the screens were missing from the windows and doors. Dirty dishes were stacked in the kitchen. Clothes were strewn all over the floor in what was apparently a bedroom for several of them.

Neither of the adults worked at a steady job, yet both were chain smoking during our visit. Beer cans littered the front yard.

The kids hovered around me as we talked, each child trying to speak louder than the other as they vied for my attention.

You get the picture. It is the picture I call "An American Tragedy," and it is too often perpetuated by ignorance, laziness, self-centeredness, and loss of any initiative.

There's plenty of "blame" to go around for these situations, but as the richest, most influential, and powerful nation in the world, we're failing far too many of our children.

And as I drove away, a sick feeling lingered in my stomach.

"The school and the church might be the only hope these kids have," I thought. "And if we don't take our jobs seriously, we're going to fail them, too.

So, let's imagine what could happen if these youngsters from this environment get on your school bus this year. The driver just happens to be "Mr. Grumpy," who treats them as if they don't matter. When they get to school and go to the cafeteria for breakfast, the lady behind the counter ignores them and scowls as they pass. Once in the classroom, they sit behind a desk while the teacher, who has been burned out for years, begins shouting assignments and just dares them to say a word.

Tragic, isn't it?

So be courageous…and do what you know you have to

do to change this scenario. As those who have been entrusted with the education, care, and nurturing of children, we have no other choice.

Because, as I have so often quoted, "Kids don't care how much we know...until they know how much we care."

CHAPTER SEVENTEEN

"Let's Teach a Lesson on Real Beauty"

"Beauty isn't about having a pretty face. It's about having a pretty mind, a pretty heart, and most importantly, a beautiful soul."

--Author Unknown

"Let's Teach a Lesson on Real Beauty"

Years ago I read a story about a beauty product company that was looking for the most beautiful woman in the world to use in their advertising. The company did some promotion on the idea, and asked local people to send a photograph and a brief essay picturing and describing an individual whom they considered to reflect the real meaning of "beautiful."

Thousands of entries were received over the next few weeks

One in particular stood out from the group, and eventually it was handed to the president of the company. It had been crudely written by a young boy from a housing project.

In the letter, he told how he was from a broken home, yet he wanted the beauty product company to know about the most beautiful woman he had ever met.

With spelling corrected, the letter read: "A beautiful woman lives down the street from me. I visit her every day. She makes me feel like I'm the most important kid in the world. We play checkers and she listens to my problems. She understands me and when I leave she always yells out the door that she's proud of me."

He continued to extol her virtues and then ended his letter with, "This picture proves to you that she is the most beautiful woman. I hope that one day I have a wife as pretty as her."

The photograph showed an elderly woman with a toothless smile sitting in a wheelchair, with her gray hair pulled back in a bun. Yet, in spite of the wrinkles that carved deep furrows on her face, one could not help but notice the piecing twinkle in her eyes.

Shaking his head and smiling, the president explained that the company would not be able to use this woman.

"She would show the world that our products aren't necessary in order to be beautiful."

Don't we, as a nation, measure beauty in such shallow, meaningless ways?

Our kids are bombarded with messages which scream that beauty must be bought in a bottle or tube and applied, or that beauty can come from a procedure, or that in order to be considered beautiful, one must dress in a provocative manner.

What foolishness! What a lie! What a deception!

Guess how many people are in the world right now. Well, according to the World Population Clock, we are quickly approaching seven billion! Yes…seven billion!

And, you know what? There are not any two of them who are 100 percent alike. Out of all the people on the face of the earth right now, no two look exactly alike…nor act alike…nor think alike…nor have the uniqueness of anyone else who is now living, or used to be living!

Amazing, isn't it? And why our students are led to believe that beauty can only look a certain way is simply ridiculous.

Man has not yet developed a method of measuring either inward or outer beauty, but personally, it's one more thing we don't need.

For real beauty can be seen every day through one's kindness, one's love for others, the unselfish gift of sharing, or the smile that wipes away the stress of another.

And as educators, we have the most unique opportunity in the world to let all of our students realize the natural beauty they possess. Encourage them. Listen to them. Give them your undivided attention. Tell them that they are uniquely beautiful.

And, above all, teach them their worth.

I love what Ann Landers wrote years ago in one of her advice columns: "Keep in mind that the true measure of an individual is how he treats a person who can do him absolutely no good."

So, throughout all our days, let us be thankful and ever mindful of the beauty that surrounds us every day, and remember that real beauty is that which always comes first from the heart.

CHAPTER EIGHTEEN

"The Day I Got the Easy Word in the Spelling Bee"

"It is a poor mind that can think
of only one way to spell a word."

-- Andrew Jackson

"The Day I Got the Easy Word in the Spelling Bee"

As the annual spelling bee came to a close in Mr. Lowe's sixth grade classroom, I was suddenly aware that there were only two of us left in the competition. It was either going to be me or Fielding Early, who just happened to be the smartest kid I had ever met.

And at that very moment, I panicked. Thoughts raced through my mind faster than a locomotive.

"What? Me and Fielding Early? I don't have a prayer!"

"Cloud," the pronouncer said as he turned my direction. "Your word is 'cloud.'"

"Cloud," I repeated?

"That's correct. 'Cloud.'"

Immediately I thought, "This is too easy! 'Cloud?' You've got to be kidding!"

"Can you give me the definition?" I heard myself saying.

A few snickers were heard at the back of the room.

The pronouncer glanced toward the sounds as he

calmly said, "A visible body of very fine water droplets or ice particles suspended in the atmosphere at altitudes ranging up to several miles."

"I heard him right," I thought. "Too easy!!!!"

"C...L...U...O...D!" I announced with all the authority in the world.

"Ding!"

"What? There must be some mistake! Didn't they hear me right?"

Groans and snickers throughout the room.

Then, the moderator turned to my opponent and announced that if he could correctly spell the word, he would be our winner.

"Cloud," Fielding repeated. Then he added, "I won't be needing a definition."

Snickers from most of the students.

It's 'C...L...O...U...D."

"Mr. Early, *you* are our champion. Congratulations!"

To this day, I cringe every time I hear that word.

Would you like to know the most commonly misspelled word by high school students? It's "their."

And that is followed by #2, "too" and #3, "receive."
"There" is #4.

And, how many times have we spelled "all right" as
"alright?"

But, every day in classrooms across America, students
misspell the most common words and the entire
meaning of the sentence is changed.

For example, what about the student who wrote: "In
Pittsburgh they manufacture iron and steal."
Hopefully, the teacher had taught about iron and
'steel."

After a film about William IV, the student's book report
wrote about the elaborate funeral he was given at his
death.

"It was a lovely funeral. It took six men to carry the
beer."

I'm certain he meant 'bier,' but maybe not.

My favorite was discovered recently while driving here
in the little town where we live. As I came to a stop
sign, I noticed that someone had written a message on
it with what appeared to be white shoe polish.

It read: "Your a lozer."

What? A 'lozer?' What in the world did that mean?

And then it hit me. The author meant "You're a loser!"

What I would have given to catch the individual that did that and teach him that if he is going to live in our little town and if he is going to be representative of the kind of education our public schools are providing, that the *least* he can do is to learn to correctly spell his graffiti!

Oh, well. Like me trying to spell "cloud," he probably just panicked and accidentally misspelled it!

I don't know if the individual who wrote the graffiti is a "loser" or not, but the one thing I am sure of, is that he is definitely *not* a 'lozer."

And that is "alright!"

CHAPTER NINETEEN

"A Christmas Story"

"When we recall Christmas past, we usually find the simplest things - not the great occasions - give off the greatest glow of happiness."

-- Bob Hope

"A Christmas Story"

Christmas. I just love it! I'm not sure that one should ever grow tired of this blessed time of year!

Such wonderful memories linger in my mind about this time of the year. My Dad was German—full blooded, as he always said. And in 1957, my mom, who is a mixture of who knows what, felt obligated to make him a German chocolate cake for Christmas.

Dad kept saying, "I'm not sure what that is. I don't remember Momma ever making one of those."

Of course, I learned much later that German chocolate cakes never originated in Germany. It actually got its name from an American named Sam German who worked for the Baker's Chocolate Company.

And, believe it or not, the first published recipe for German's chocolate cake appeared in the Dallas Morning News in the mid fifties.

But, Mother had gotten the recipe at the beauty shop and she was determined that it would be part of our Christmas dinner that year.

Oh, and what a sacrifice to make such a cake back then. Like many of you remember, there wasn't any extra money for such frills. But, with determination and frugality, she gradually collected all the ingredients—

coconut, pecans, sugar, chocolate, and more chocolate.

A few days before Christmas, she ordered us all out of the kitchen, and began the arduous task of making that cake. I can remember smelling that remarkable, tantalizing, mouth-watering smell as it wafted through the little two-bedroom house we called home. I couldn't wait for my first taste of that cake. Time hadn't just slowed down. I was convinced that it had stopped altogether.

Sometime just before noon, mom announced that the cake was ready. My sister and I nearly knocked each other down as we ran to the kitchen. Daddy was close behind. It was as if we were about to witness something we would never forget.

I almost expected the heavenly hosts to begin singing. Trumpets should have been blaring. A ray of sunlight came through the kitchen window and fell upon those four layers of heavenly bliss as it sat there in the middle of the kitchen stove.

"O-h-h-h-h," was all we kids could utter. It was spectacular! Our eyes were as big as saucers as we tried to comprehend the majesty of this moment. Visions of sugarplums dancing in our heads didn't hold a candle to this beauty.

"Sit down, sit down," Mom said. "I'll bring it to the table and you all can have a bite. But don't expect too big of a piece, 'cause we're saving this for Christmas dinner."

We all minded. Faster than you could say "semi-sweet chocolate," we were there at the kitchen table. Mom turned around to the stove to pick up her masterpiece. What a creation she had made!

You've seen those scenes in movies that are done in slow motion? Well, just picture it now. There's momma, turning around with that glorious cake resting atop her very best clear plate. We're all smiling. It's a scene right out of "It's a Wonderful Life."

And then, for who knows what reason, momma hit a wet spot on the floor. That right foot started to slide and momma was suddenly doing contortions we never dreamed possible. A look of disbelief crossed her face as she lost her grip on the cake and it slowly started a rapid ascent toward the ceiling. Almost as quickly, it started its descent. We were no help. We just sat there, with our mouths hanging open and followed that cake from blastoff to landing.

And land, it did. Upside down... in the middle of the kitchen floor.

The next thing I remember, we were all sitting around a chocolate mess that seemed to have exploded. We were all four in the floor, hugging one another. Momma was crying. Dad was comforting her. Sis and I were hugging both of them.

Sis said something like, "Don't cry, Momma. I never liked chocolate anyway." What a lie!

Through her tears, Mom started picking up the pieces and trying to salvage as much as she could.

"Don't worry, Momma," I said. " We'll just, we'll just… eat it off the floor. Look… it still tastes good. We'll just sit here and eat it! We don't care."

Daddy finally said, "Listen, honey, of all the cakes I've ever eaten, this is the one I'll always remember. We all will. Because this was truly a gift given from the heart and those are always the best kind."

I never forgot that day. It's as if it happened just yesterday. And… to this day… I don't eat German chocolate cake. There's never been another one that could even come close to matching the exquisite, delectable, indescribably delicious taste of the one my momma baked during the Christmas holidays in 1957 that our family ate off of the kitchen floor.

CHAPTER
TWENTY

*"Yes, we'll take those kids ...
for better or for worse."*

"Live so that when your children think of
fairness, caring, and integrity,
they think of you."

--H. Jackson Brown

"Yes, we'll take those kids... for better or for worse."

We've all heard the traditional wedding vows scores of times.

"Will you take this man/woman for better or for worse?"

Yet, those words always cause me to think about just what a commitment we are making when we utter them. I suspect that, like me, most of the guests are reaffirming their vows along with the bride and groom.

And, whether we want to admit it or not, taking on the role of working with children in our schools is much the same.

We accept the challenge... for better... or worse.

A few days ago I met a 16-year old kid who told me that he had just moved in with his grandmother and grandfather.

It didn't take long to realize that this young man's world was caving in on him.

It seems that his parents were getting a divorce. Their home had to be sold. The mother could only afford a place large enough for her and her two younger children. The dad had moved in with his girlfriend.

So, he did the only thing he knew to do. He picked up the phone and called his grandparents who lived about a hundred miles away. They told him they would leave immediately and that he could live with them.

Now think about this for a moment.

Think about when *you* were sixteen years old.

Try to remember how immature and frightened you were of so many things, yet didn't want anyone to know it.

Try to imagine how you might dread changing schools. How the thought of leaving your friends of many years was devastating.

Think about how it must be to "start life over" at sixteen years of age.

Wow!

I can't imagine.

Historically, according to the National Survey of America's Families, the number of children in the care of their grandparents has fluctuated between 1.3 and 2.1 percent of all children between 1940 and the present. Now that may not sound like a huge number, but when you consider that there are currently over sixty million youngsters between the ages of 5 – 19, you can quickly compute that the number of children in the care of their grandparents is over a million youngsters!

I simply say, thank heaven for caring grandparents who are willing to assume, once again, the important role of parenting.

As educators, we should be cognizant of the impact that these changes in a child's family often make on the student.

I recently read an article by Archibald Hart which dealt with the feelings that youngsters often have following such a dramatic change in the family.

According to Hart, the following is often the case:

1. The child often feels alone and frightened due to the collapse of the family structure that he/she has known. That loneliness can often be acute and long remembered.

2. Children are often pulled by love and loyalty to their parents in both directions.

3. Uncertainty about the future often causes deep-seated insecurity in children.

4. When anger and resentment between parents is prevalent in a divorce, it often creates intense fear in the child.

5. It is not uncommon for children to take upon themselves anxiety concerning their parents. They worry intensely about their mother in particular, with the departure of the father being a frightening event.

6. When a move for the child is involved, depression is almost inevitable.

Dr. Lee Salk, a prominent child psychologist, has said, "The trauma of divorce is second only to death. Children sense a deep loss and feel they are suddenly vulnerable to forces beyond their control."

I realize that for many, divorce is a last resort, and is sometimes unavoidable.

But as administrators and teachers, we can help make a difficult situation better by being aware of the critical needs of the student during this time.

May I offer the following list of suggestions adapted from a list by Dr. Steve Stephens:

1. Be there for the child. The very presence of a caring individual is calming.

2. Speak gently and confidently. The student is desperate for consolation.

3. Listen. Let them tell you about their fears no matter how irrational. Be attentive and patient.

4. Give them a positive focus. Students are often most

vulnerable during this time and a positive role-model can do much to reassure the child.

5. Emphasize to them that there is always a way out. Although this change in their life hurts immensely, time will lessen the pain.

6. Remind them that we all have fears.

As educators, we have an awesome responsibility in helping to meet the needs of today's students. But in spite of that, I hope that we recognize that sometimes the most important lesson that we can teach is the one that shows a student just how much we care... during the good times *and* the bad.

It is truly one lesson that they will never forget.

"When I stand before God at the end of my life, I would hope that I would not have a single bit of talent left, and could say, 'I used everything You gave me.'"

--Erma Bombeck

CHAPTER TWENTY-ONE

"Disruptive Child? Who ya' Gonna Call?"

There can be no keener revelation
of a society's soul than the way in which
it treats its children."

-- Nelson Mandela

"Disruptive Child? Who ya' Gonna Call?"

I read with interest about an Indiana elementary school calling the local police and having a six-year-old child arrested for "assaulting" the principal.

What? I couldn't believe what I was reading.

According to the police report, school officials reported that the child had kicked the principal and told him and the assistant principal that he was "going to kill them."

"The student was yelling and screaming and lying on the floor when police arrived," the report said.

As I continued to read, I became even more surprised at the staggering statistics dealing with students who have been arrested.

Between 2009 and 2010, over 90,000 students were arrested in Albuquerque, New Mexico alone. But wait. It gets even more alarming. In our beloved state of Texas, there were over 300,000 students who were given misdemeanors in 2010 as a result of their inappropriate behavior while in school. That number included children as young as six years old.

What are some of the behaviors that are giving our kids a police record before they even graduate? Charges include an amazing range of crimes for those youngsters under the age of 13. For example, offenses include spraying cologne on another student, giving "wedgies," or having a food fight.

And one six-year-old was charged with sexual assault by school officials during a recess game of tag. In order to get the sexual assault charge removed from his school records, the parents hired a lawyer to "prove that the charge had no legal basis."

Wow! Now that's troubling!

Oh, I don't want to start playing the blame game. There's enough of that for all of us – schools, parents, and society in general.

None of us want confrontation. Too many parents choose to ignore the problem in order to avoid confrontation. Schools have been handed the problems. And yes, at some point, we're beaten down and reach out to a more powerful authority.

Of course, there are no easy answers. But one that is showing a great deal of promise is that of giving children responsibility at an early age.

Over a 40-year period, one study followed the lives of 456 teenage boys from inner-city Boston. Many of them came from poor and impoverished homes. "Regardless of intelligence, family income, ethnic background or amount of education," if the boys had been given responsibilities, such as jobs, chores around the house, etc., they had been happier, more successful, and more productive as adults.

I'm old enough now to remember that parents of yesteryear were extremely permissive. They permitted their children to work, to have responsibilities, and to follow the examples set by the parents.

Simply put, I believe that we could all do more for our children by not doing so much for them.

We've all seen kids being given too much. Too much idle time, too many toys, too many inappropriate games, too much television, too much access to violence. The list is practically endless.

I once saw a quote that simply said, "Some parents begin by giving in and end with giving up."

Let's all vow to work at being more sensitive to their needs and frustrations. Let's commit to listening with interest and understanding. Let us remember our fears when we were children and how a sympathetic adult helped us through a difficult time. Strive to be more patient and helpful as they are growing and developing. Let us allow them to make mistakes without belittling. Commit to a life of encouragement for them. And by all means, be a positive role-model for the students you serve.

And when all else fails, a loving, gentle approach will often work wonders.

As someone once wisely wrote, "The trouble with the

problem child is not always apparent -- sometimes it's two parents.

CHAPTER TWENTY-TWO

"Patience and Gentleness: *Lessons Learned from a Child*"

"By learning, you will teach.
By teaching, you will learn."

-- Latin Proverb

Patience and Gentleness:
Lessons learned from a child

As I stood at the foot of the bed where a 23-year old girl lay in the trauma ward of the hospital, I couldn't help but be overwhelmed by the tubes, the ventilator, the monitors, the variety of life-giving nourishment that dripped into this practically lifeless body. Only hours before, a car accident had left her vehicle crushed like a wad of paper and the fact that she was alive at all could only be called a miracle.

I thought back to an earlier time, when this young lady was only some eight or nine years old. There she was in our backyard, watching the birds as they consumed the seeds from the feeder. A squirrel or two had ventured down from a tree limb overhead, and ventured cautiously to the growing mound of seeds that had been knocked to the ground.

The squirrels would take a sunflower seed with their two front paws, then sit up tall and begin working to get to the small morsel that lay inside.

Fascinating.

With her eyes wide with excitement, she turned to me and whispered.

"Can you put a few seeds in my hand?"

I nodded, reached my hand into the plastic bag of sunflower seeds, and placed a few into her small hand.

Cautiously, she began to bend down to the lawn, and ever so slowly, began to inch toward the squirrel.

"No way," I thought to myself. "There's no way that either of those squirrels is going to eat out of her hand. But, hey, she's a kid. Let her discover that for herself."

I signaled for those inside to watch. All eyes were on her as she crept forward, moving only a few inches, then stopping. Not a muscle was moving. Then the process was started over again.

Suddenly, the squirrel closest to her stopped eating and turned to looked at her. He cocked his head from side to side and I don't think that I was imagining a quizzical look that came upon his face.

By now, she was about three feet from him. Patiently, she inched even closer. Her right arm began to be extended toward the squirrel.

Then, much to the amazement of all of us, the squirrel took a small jump toward her and began eating from her hand! I could not believe my eyes.

Here was a gentle girl, who loved animals of every kind. It was as if she understood them and they knew that they were safe with her.

A few years after this incident, she left high school as a sophomore to attend college through a special program for gifted math and science students. A few more years and she had easily earned her bachelor's degree. Her hope for a gentler, most caring world was evidenced by the way she lived.

And then, at age 23, she and her husband were involved in a terrific, unimaginable accident. For weeks, she hung on to life by a thread. Her recovery was slow. Her treatments and surgeries were many.

We later learned that the doctors had discovered that her right leg was broken in several places. The right arm was broken, her kneecap shattered. The collar bone and sternum were broken. Her lung was punctured, along with her liver. Even the fingers on her right hand were shattered.

But in spite of this, this gentle human being did not lose her hope, but continued to make a difference. The doctors, nurses, specialists to this day are astounded.

This life-changing accident, which happened only a week before Christmas, made all of us realize the precious gift of life, the importance of family and friends, and the uncertainty of tomorrow.

So, our dear niece, we shall continue to hold you in our hearts and in our prayers and look forward to a time when perhaps, because of your example, we will each have the patience and gentleness to feed God's creatures from our own hands.

"Do not educate a child to be rich. Educate him to be happy, so that when he grows up, he'll know the value of things, not the price."

--Author Unknown

CHAPTER TWENTY-THREE

The Day My Sister and I Laughed 'til We Cried

Remember me with smiles and laughter, for that is how I will remember you all. If you can only remember me with tears, then don't remember me at all.

-- Laura Ingalls Wilder

The Day My Sister and I Laughed 'til We Cried

Did you ever do or say something really stupid? Come on, be honest. Remember when you said something really dumb before you even thought through it? Well, I hope you ended up by laughing at yourself…and I hope you laughed louder than anyone.

We've all done it! And at our family gatherings, those are the things that bring such laughter each time we're together. Making stupid mistakes has become some of the best family memories ever!

My sister and I have always enjoyed a good laugh, whether at ourselves…or at the other one.

She recently called and was just laughing hysterically when I answered the phone.

"Riney, I have just done the dumbest thing ever…"

And the story began. Remember now, she could barely tell this story for all the laughing that took place between each phrase.

She began recounting the story of how the Governor of Illinois had been reportedly trying to sell the Senate seat of Barack Obama.

"I've been hearing about this for days," she said, "and I just couldn't believe that he thought he could get away with that!"

When a couple of ladies from her neighborhood came over for a morning cup of coffee and a visit, the subject came up.

"I told the ladies that I just thought he had to be the dumbest man I had ever heard of to think that he could sell Obama's seat," she reported. "Doesn't he know that it's against the law to do that?"

One of the ladies nodded in agreement while the other said, "He does have his nerve, doesn't he?"

"Why, yes he has his nerve," sister Shirley responded. "Doesn't he know that Obama's seat is owned by the government, and you can't sell any of the furniture in the nation's capitol, even if it is just one chair!"

At that point, the ladies both put on a confused look, and then one of them started chuckling. That's all it took, and the other one burst into laughter.

"Shirley, it's not Obama's chair that the Governor is taking bids on....it's his Senate *position* he's trying to sell!"

Shirley and I were both in tears of laughter as the story ended.

———

"How could I be that stupid?" she asked.

"Well, since you told your story, I'll tell mine," I said.

I told her that a few days ago I had been watching one of the pro-football games on television, and at the end of the game the announcer began reporting which players had been selected to participate on the 'Pro Bowl' team.

As I listened, I mentioned to my wife Karen, 'Those poor football players. They make them play golf sometimes with the pros…and now they're making them participate with other football players in a game of bowling! When is it going to end?"

There was a moment of silence, and then a knee-slapping laugh, followed by "You've got to be kidding! It's not a bowling match…it's football in a 'bowl' game! Remember? Cotton *Bowl*. Orange *Bowl*. Rose ..."

"I get it! I get it!" I yelled.

Immediately, I realized how ridiculous my assumption had been. And, the only thing I could do was to laugh at myself.

My sister thoroughly enjoyed my story, and we acknowledged that we were "even" on really stupid comments.

Two wrongs did make it right!

As Elsa Maxwell once said, "Laugh at yourself first, before anyone else can."

And that's good advice!

CHAPTER
TWENTY-FOUR

Above and Beyond the
Call of Duty

Don't ask yourself what the world needs;
ask yourself what makes you come alive.
And then go and do that.
Because what the world needs are people
who have come alive.

-- Harold Whitman

"Above and Beyond the Call of Duty"

I've never seen it on an application before. I don't think I've ever heard it asked during an interview. But if there was a way to find out if an individual was accustomed to going "above and beyond" what was expected, wouldn't they most likely make an incredible employee?

"Above and beyond the call of duty" is the way most of us have heard it. I actually "googled" it, and found that there were over 968,000 references to that remark. And I discovered that it is an "idiom." I've actually used that word a few times when describing someone I thought was a complete moron. But basically, "above and beyond the call of duty" means "one who does much more than is expected."

One reference gave examples, i.e. "if your waiter goes beyond the call of duty, leave a bigger tip." I agree with that.

Folks who research this type of thing will tell you that it was first used in reference to police officers, fire fighters, or soldiers who were injured or killed while doing their jobs.

Well, I think we need to add "educators" to that list. Lately, it seems, I've been hearing more and more stories from teachers who routinely go "above and beyond the call of duty."

Take, for example, a third-grade teacher who recently took a day of her Christmas holidays to attend the funeral of the mother of one of her students. During a time of year when kids should get to sleep late, stay up late, play outside, look forward to surprises, this little girl got the biggest surprise of all. Right at Christmas, her mother dies.

And even on such a short notice, the teacher left her own family, and drove across town to an unfamiliar neighborhood, because she cared. Her student will never forget running to her teacher, throwing her arms around her, sobbing her little heart out.

That "policy" wasn't in the notebook that is handed out at the beginning of every school year. No where does it say that you are to be there for the students twenty-four hours a day, seven days a week, come rain or shine. It doesn't say that you have to work "over-time." No, it states that you should be able to do your job in 185 days, 7:30 a.m. to 3:30 p.m.

But there's not an educator around who has a heart for the teaching profession who believes that.

I remember Coach Gordon Wood telling me some of those "above and beyond" stories as I sat in his living room in Brownwood, Texas. At that time he had won more state championships than anybody in the country.

You know what he told me? He said, "Riney, it wasn't

just the game of football I had to teach. It was the game of life." And then, for an hour or so, he told stories of kids who needed more than just a coach…they needed someone who was willing to go "above and beyond." He said he once drove all night to drive to the Texas-Mexico border to pay the fine and get one of his students out of jail. "We had a good father/son talk for the next six hours. He was a different kid after that."

Coach Wood developed pneumonia, suffered a heart attack, and died a few months after our visit.

"Above and beyond the call of duty."

That third grade teacher did it when she made certain that she was there for that little third-grade girl.

Coach Gordon Wood did it almost daily during his forty-three seasons.

And right now, as you are reading this, there is a teacher going "above and beyond the call of duty." Oh, it might be a coach, a secretary, a principal, a custodian, a bus driver, or a superintendent, but you can bet that it happens more often than any of us realize, because they don't do it for the glory…they do it for the kids.

"Above and beyond." What a difference it would make if we all had that philosophy!

"When you are going through something hard, and wonder where God is... remember that the teacher is always quiet during a test."

--Author Unknown

CHAPTER TWENTY-FIVE

"Life: It's All About Choices"

"Consider it pure joy ... whenever you face trials of many kinds, because you know that the testing of your faith produces perseverance."

-- James 1:2-3

"Life: It's All About Choices"

As I listened to a group of educators at the end of a long school day, it suddenly occurred to me that everything they were saying was negative!

One was complaining of an entire class of students. Another was attacking another co-worker. And yet, another was complaining of policy. Goodness gracious! Wasn't there *anything* for which to be grateful?

It's really easy to get into that rut, isn't it? Lou Holtz once said, "Never tell your problems to anyone. 20% don't care and the other 80% are glad you have them."

I suspect that there may be some truth to that.

All of this complaining reminds me of the story of the teacher who brought his lunch to school every day. On Monday, he took out his bologna sandwich and ate it without any comment.

The next day, another bologna sandwich, and he immediately muttered, "I can't believe I've got bologna again."

Well, when it turned out to be bologna on the third day, he ranted, "This is ridiculous! Day after day, all I get is bologna!"

"Perhaps you should tell your wife not to make you a bologna sandwich for a few days," his co-worked responded.

"Hey, don't bring my wife into this! I make my own lunch every morning!"

Author and speaker Jim Rohn once said, "If you want things to change, then you have to change. If you want things to get better, you have to get better."

I couldn't agree more.

Our schools are often breeding places for negativity, and of all the institutions that do not need negative comments, it is our schools.

What can we do to turn some of this around?

1. *Avoid those people who drag you down with them.*

One of my favorite teachers used to remind us that "one bad apple spoils the barrel." I was a long time figuring out that she wasn't talking about apples at all.

When we are constantly being bombarded with negative comments and thoughts by those around us, we begin to make negative remarks, as well. We join right in, thinking that we're helping the situation. In nearly all cases, nothing could be farther from the truth.

2. *If you can't say something nice, don't say anything at all.*

Who among us did not repeatedly hear that from our parents? And it's absolutely the truth! Not only does it tear someone else down, it's tearing us down as well. Let's strive to be the person who is remembered as someone who always found something good to say about everybody.

3. *Your attitude is everything!*

One of the most beautiful examples I've ever read told of a young blind boy sitting along a busy street. His sign read, "I am blind. Please help."

As a gentleman walked by each day, he noticed that the boy would collect only a few coins. After dropping some money into the boy's small collection, the man picked up the sign, turned it over, and wrote a few words for others to see as they passed by.

Late that afternoon, the gentleman again walked past the young boy, and noticed that the young boy's plate was nearly running over.

"I see you're doing much, much better today," the man said.

"Yes," the boy responded. "Are you the man who rewrote my sign this morning? What did you write that has caused so many people to give money to help me?"

"I only wrote the truth, but I said it in a different way," the man answered.

The sign that had read, "I am blind. Please help," now read "Today is a beautiful day and I cannot see it."

Both signs informed the people that the boy was blind, but the new sign made them realize how blessed they were to have their sight.

Today, remember that in everything you have a choice. You can be happy or angry. You can choose to be someone who tears people down or builds them up. You can choose to thankful or ungrateful. The list is endless.

Life really is a choice, isn't it?

CHAPTER
TWENTY-SIX

"Oh, yes, George Bailey!
It's a wonderful life!"

"And in the end,
it's not the years in your life that count.
It's the life in your years."

--Abraham Lincoln

"Oh, yes, George Bailey! It's a wonderful life!"

Oh, how I love that line from "It's a Wonderful Life," where Clarence the angel says: "Strange, isn't it? Each man's life touches so many other lives, and when he isn't around he leaves an awful hole, doesn't he?"

Wow! Now that's good stuff!

Poor George Bailey has gone through a rough day and he'd just had it. Finally, when he was at his lowest point, leaning on a bridge railing, he began praying: "I want to live again. I want to live again. Please, God, let me live again."

At that point I lose it. Haven't we all been there? We just feel like the world is against us and that the situation seems helpless.

But, my, oh my. If we'd just remember all those folks who are depending on us. Did you ever stop to think about how many lives have been changed because of you?

Come on now. Don't be so modest. The truth is: there are more than you will ever know!

I began thinking recently about those individuals who have so profoundly shaped my own life. Wow! Have I been blessed! So many who believed in me, encouraged me, opened doors for me, walked along side of me, and helped me to become the person that I am today.

Of course, parents immediately come to mind. I'm so thankful for my Mom and Dad and the values that they instilled in each of their children. My mom, who died at 86 years of age, always had such a positive outlook on things. Her sense of humor is off the scale! My Dad, who passed away at 80 years of age, was a soft-spoken, gentle man who helped so many people with his servant spirit. I'm so glad that they were around to touch my life.

And, God then gave me an incredible wife who is truly the "wind beneath my wings." Now that I spend so many days on the road speaking to educators, she is always there with me. I often feel that it's as if she walks me to the stage, then steps back behind the curtain, and the spotlight falls on me. If only the audience knew how it was that I really got to this point! Yes…she's touched my life.

And I owe so much to so many others. One in particular who will forever be on my list of influential giants is Dr. O. C. "Mike" Taylor. Oh, I wish you all knew this man like I know him. Underneath what appeared to be a rough and gruff exterior, lived a man whose passion was to make a difference in the lives of the people he loved.

I shall never forget him calling me into his office and

giving me a list of things that were about to happen. One, I was going to get my master's degree. Two, I was going to become a principal. Three, he was going to see that it happened.

And "see that it happened," … he did! Within hours, I was a principal. Within eighteen months, I finished my degree. And all along the way, he was there to encourage me, to direct me, and to foster me.

Unashamedly, I say, "I love that man!"

Yes, it is strange isn't it? Each person's life touches so many other lives.

So, what are you waiting for? Today, touch a life. Make a difference. I believe that God put you where you are for a purpose.

And just like George Bailey, you'll discover that you can "live again."

And what a wonderful life that can be.

"Perhaps our eyes need to be washed by our
tears once in a while,
so that we can see life
with a clearer view again."

-- Alex Tan

CHAPTER TWENTY-SEVEN

"God Bless
Our Border Kids!"

"I just know that somewhere in this world
someone is happy with a whole lot less
than we have."

-- Author Unknown

God Bless Our Border Kids

I'll never forget doing a training session in a school a few years ago which was only a stones throw away from Mexico. I remember asking if there were any children who crossed the Rio Grande to attend classes there?

"Oh, sure," the principal softly answered. "They never miss. They turn in every assignment. And they're probably more eager to learn than any students we have."

My opinion of this controversial topic was changed that day.

I once read an article in the about children in Texas schools who are being so dramatically affected by the violence of the drug problems along our borders and in our cities and communities.

For example, in El Paso, classroom teachers have begun explaining to students about the stages of psychological trauma experienced by victims of brutal attacks. Many children of all ages have experienced such violence first-hand as a result of drug-related incidences in that area of Texas.

A 17-year old student told the class, "I've been through all three stages: impact, recoil, and reorganization of my life." Then he broke down into tears as he was talking and sobbed, "My mom goes in and out of recoil stage."

One teacher compared what is happening in our border towns to the same that's occurring in Iraq and Afghanistan.

In fact, Texas law enforcement officials recently confirmed that several Mexican drug cartels are using children to help in their smuggling operations.

Can you imagine! The gangs out of Mexico have an unbelievable name they have attached to the children who do this work for them. They simply refer to them as "the expendables."

"The expendables!" It is unthinkable that someone could be so heartless, so insensitive, as to consider a child as "expendable," and care nothing for their safety!

Another recent study was done regarding children who unsuccessfully tried to enter the United States, but were carried back across the bridge and returned to Mexican authorities.

It is estimated that between fifty and one-hundred thousand children are returned to Mexico and other Central American countries each year. What happens to them? Your guess is as good as mine, but estimates are that as many as one-third of them never get reunited with their families.

This is why, more than ever, our classrooms have to focus on caring about our students.

The welfare of our students must become our schools number one priority.

A teacher recently told me that she vowed that school year to focus first and foremost on her relationship with her students, and then, on academics.

"It's been amazing," she told me, "but the learning of the subject matter seems to have come so much easier this year. I think it is because, for the first time in my teaching career, I've put them first, and they know it, and I believe they want to please me.

"And," she continued, "because I know what is going on in most of their lives, I'm looking at them in a whole new light. I've come to realize that these students have got issues at home and outside of this school that are huge. They now know that I'm here for them!"

I feel so strongly about this issue. I encourage you to work with parents, with co-workers, with other adults, to convey the concept that before learning can take place, relationships must be established.

If you have doubts, think about your own experiences. In almost every case, the teacher you remember as being the most effective and the one you considered your favorite, was the one you knew cared about you the most.

So, I encourage you to make it your resolve to work on relationships, to genuinely care about those you serve, and to realize that our own real joy in life comes from making a difference in the lives of others.

For at this very moment, there's a border kid praying that someone like you or me will cross his path and his life will forever be changed.

TWENTY-EIGHT

"If You Gotta' Have a Graduation Ceremony, at Least Make it Memorable!"

"It is bad to suppress laughter.
It goes back down to your hips."

-- Author Unknown

"If you gotta have a graduation ceremony, at least make it memorable"

There's nothing quite like a high school graduation.

And one of the most memorable nights of my life happened the night I graduated from Brownwood High School in central Texas.

Even with only about 180 graduates, there was nothing in town large enough to hold the crowd, except the high school stadium.

As we started gathering around 7:00 p.m. for the traditional 8:00 p.m. graduation, the sky was beginning to turn a deep, dark blue-green color. The band, minus all the seniors, made a meager attempt at *Pomp and Circumstance* as we marched along the front of the bleachers and turned to take our rightful spot on the make-shift stage which had been set up in the middle of the football field on the fifty-yard line.

The next indication we all had that something wasn't going well were the sudden gusts of wind that began blowing. During the Superintendent's opening remarks, a potted palm blew over. Then another. You could hear the murmur of the crowd as every eye panned the darkening sky.

The pastor of the First Baptist Church was called to the podium. He had just started his prayer when a bolt of lightning and a crack of thunder shook the entire stadium. The preacher sounded like a record as if he shifted from 33 1/3 RPM to 78 RPM, and the next word I heard was a quick "Amen!"

"Run! Run for the auditorium!" the Superintendent immediately began yelling. "Hurry!"

The superintendent knew as well as we did that something nearby had been struck by lightning, and none of us were willing to wait around to see if we were next.

Then, without warning, the rain came. And it came in torrents! The girls, with their "big Texas hair" only moments before, now looked like they had just stepped out of the shower. As the rain pelted our maroon graduation gowns, maroon dye started running down our arms and necks. White shirts were immediately transformed into what, in later years, would be known as the "tie-dye" look.

And then, like a stampeding herd of West Texas cattle, the seniors, the band, the parents, the staff, and the guests, started running across the football field, heading for safety in an auditorium that had only a couple of hundred seats.

Well, you can imagine the chaos. Only a few lucky

guests got into the hot, stuffy enclosure. Many of the grandparents, aunts, uncles, and friends collapsed in the hallway, while newly-appointed monitors kept insisting that only parents and graduating seniors would be allowed inside.

With no air conditioning, the windows were cracked just enough to get a breeze blowing across the drenched, "still-in-a-state-of-shock" crowd.

Once the graduates were assembled on the first ten or twelve rows of seats, the Superintendent made another attempt to start the ceremony.

"Well, this has really been an exciting evening," he said as he took a deep breath. At some point, he had unconscientiously loosened his tie. His shirttail was hanging out in the back, his hair was standing in every direction, and he was panting. All of this, of course, as he tried his best to appear calm.

Almost at that exact moment, we started smelling smoke, and moments later heard the sound of sirens screaming between bursts of thunder and lightning.

The high school principal run onto the stage, whispered something in the superintendent's ear. A shocked, disbelieving look came over his face.

"Oh, my goodness. The old community center downtown is burning to the ground!"

Well, many couldn't resist the opportunity to see the

oldest wooden structure in Brown County on fire, so many got up and hurried to the nearest exits. The empty seats were quickly refilled by grandmothers and aunts.

So, on a dreary evening in late May, 1960, the graduating class of Brownwood High School experienced one of the most exciting graduation ceremonies ever.

We never knew for certain if lightning had struck the building, or if some disgruntled sophomore had decided to make a bonfire out of that old 1940s WPA project.

One good thing: none of the graduating seniors were suspects. For once, we all had an alibi.

My memorable graduation is equaled only by the one that took place in Grapevine, Texas during the 1980's. It seems someone had forgotten to turn off the stadium sprinkler system and it came on about halfway through the service.

But we'll save that story for another day.

TWENTY-NINE

"Why I Will Never Forget Christina"

"Anyone who does anything
to help a child in his life
is a hero to me. "

-- Fred Rogers

"Why I Will Never Forget Christina"

Christina had made plans all week to attend a special event on Saturday.

"I can't wait for Saturday," she told her friends. "I get to meet one of my role models."

This bright, talented third grader was an amazing little girl.

"I was born on one of the worst days in America," she would tell folks when they met her for the first time.

"Yes, I was born on September 11, 2001. You know, 9/11."

She would go on to tell you that she had been featured in a book, "Faces of Hope," which had featured one baby from each of the fifty states who was born that fateful day when 3,000 people lost their lives in New York City.

Christina had asked for a guitar on Christmas this past year. She loved music and her latest goal was to learn to play that instrument.

I can only imagine the squeals of glee on Christmas morning when the one item she had wanted so badly was there under the tree. She spent much of that day beginning to learn to play the various chords.

"I also love baseball," she told everyone. "I'm hoping to be the first female professional baseball player."

She was well on her way to this dream, as she was the only girl on her Little League team where she played second baseman. No doubt the love of the game had come from her father who was a baseball scout, and a grandfather who had managed the Philadelphia Phillies, as well the New York Mets and Yankees.

 This amazing young girl seemed to excel at everything. One of Christina's favorite pastimes was swimming with her older brother, Dallas. Although he was two years older, they appeared to be best friends and were "inseparable" according to those who knew them both.

Her teachers would tell you that Christina was good at everything, perhaps because she was interested in everything. Singing, dancing, civics, animals, gymnastics … the list was practically endless. Once a week you would find her singing in her church choir.

One of her favorite charities was called "Kids Helping Kids," and this group helped fulfill her unbelievable desire to help others.

And for a nine-year-old third grader, she was already making big plans for her future.

"I want to attend Penn State," she had recently told her

parents. "and I want to study about helping people who are less fortunate. Or, I might be a veterinarian or a politician."

Yes, everyone agreed. Christina was an amazing young girl.

Saturday arrived and her Dad hurried to the kitchen to prepare one of her favorite items for breakfast, a bacon and cheese omelet.

A neighbor had agreed to take her to meet this new role model, a young politician who was going to be speaking at a local rally.

And on Saturday, January 8, 2011, little Christina Green, who had recently been elected to serve on her elementary school's student council, was driven to the grocery parking lot to shake hands and meet her heroine, U.S. Rep. Gabrielle Giffords.

By now, we have all heard of the terrible aftermath at a Safeway parking lot in Tucson, Arizona, when a lone gunman began firing. Six people were killed, including Christina.

Her father would later describe her as "vibrant," and his "little Princess."

And, as I listened to an interview with her mother and father in the days after the shooting, my heart grieved, as did so many others.

Of course, we'll never really understand why someone could so senselessly take the life of another, especially of someone so young.

As educators, I believe that our greatest strength lies in our compassion for others, especially children. Our God-given ability to nurture them, to encourage them, and to help them discover their own purpose is nothing short of a gift.

So today, whether it's one of your students, or one of your children, a spouse, or any loved one, take time to let them know you care about them.

Yes, we're all busy with test scores, and new programs, and adjusting to change, but there are some things that should remain constant.

And, as it has been so perfectly stated, "The greatest of these is love."

THIRTY

"If I Could
Start My Own School"

They may forget what you said but they will never forget how you made them feel."

-- Carol Buchner

"If I Could Start My Own School"

Did you ever wonder what a school would look like if you could do everything just like you wanted? What would your philosophy be? What rules would you have? If you could build what you felt would be the "perfect" school, what would you do differently, if anything, from things you've done in the past?

Well, when a group of educators get together, we often have plenty of ideas on what's right, what wrong, and what we would do differently if given the opportunity.

Now, before you get all defensive, just remember that these are my ideas and they might not agree with yours. Some of them are based on my own experiences; others on my belief system. Many of them are subject to parents and teachers supporting the same ideas -- and we know how difficult that can be, don't we?

Nevertheless, I hope it gets you to thinking about what you think is important.

If I had my own school...

... We would only have teachers who loved teaching, loved their students, and were passionate about the profession. How would I judge that? *You just know*!!! After all, kids know who the best teachers are…and in our hearts, we do too.

… Teachers would be paid salaries commensurate with doctors and lawyers, because after all, they are doing one of the most important jobs in the world.

… Children would memorize basic math facts. Yes…memorize! When they heard 7 X 8, for example, the answer 56 would be spontaneous and instant.

… We would read, read, read! That's the way I think we learn…and the more we read, the more we know.

… Teachers would be able to discipline the students. If parents didn't want their children disciplined, their kids would have to be taught elsewhere.

… We would start every day with a pledge and a prayer. I know what you're thinking: *"Why, you can't pray in school."* Remember, this is MY school, and parents who brought their children there would be doing so because they support that idea, too. If you don't like prayer in school, start your own. Oh…on second thought, we already have those schools, don't we?

… Kids would move at their own rate. Yep, I know some of you think that it's a relatively new idea, but not really. In fact, if you look back at the turn-of-the-century to one-room schools, kids moved at their own rate, and older kids would often teach them, thus reinforcing what they had already learned.

… We'd go to school year-round, and the kids could take a couple of weeks anytime during the year to take trips with their parents, visit grandparents, etc. And, they wouldn't be counted absent because the value of family time together is paramount.

… All children would learn at least one foreign language, and learn it well.

… Students would learn basic keyboarding skills beginning in kindergarten. This is a lifetime skill and should be second-nature to all of us by the time we reached second or third grade..

… Values, such as honesty, integrity, kindness, compassion, truthfulness, and morality would be a big part of every day's instruction. And, we would use stories to illustrate these virtues. The next time that a teacher or preacher or lecturer begins telling a story, notice that people invariably begin to look up and listen. We all love a good story!

… Every child would have their own computer and know how to effectively search for any information they needed.

… Uniforms would be required. I hate the classification of youngsters because of what their parents can afford for them to wear.

… Parents would be required to be involved in their

children's education and be active participants.

Oh, I could go on and on, but those are some of the most important issues as far as I am concerned. Until my imaginary school is up and running, let's support what we've got by encouraging teachers, providing the very best leadership for them, and providing meaningful and worthwhile education to the children to whom we are entrusted.

For as Barbara Harrell Carson is quoted as saying: "Students learn what they care about, from people they care about and who, they know, care about them . . ."

Hey, that's *my* school!

In closing...

Gosh, I hope you enjoyed this second book!

If you did, I'd love to hear from you. Just e-mail me a note to riney@yahoo.com and let me know what you thought.

I'm still more surprised than anyone that God has given me the opportunities that He has.

And, looking back, I realize more and more each day that He put people in my path to steer me through life and to help me make choices that He knew all along!

What amazing, gentle, loving, caring parents! For that, I am so thankful!

And then came my gentle, loving, caring wife! Homerun! Thank you, Lord!

My years as a radio announcer would never have happened if it had not been for my friend, Bob Taylor, who told me that they were needing an announcer at the local radio station where he worked. He told them that I would be good at that, so they said, "Have him here on Saturday afternoon to start working!" Wow! I got the job, although I really never even applied. That was a God thing, you know.

Then, when I started teaching, God put so many

amazing people in my path, like Dr. O. C. "Mike" Taylor who told me rather emphatically that I was going to be a principal. And, sure enough, I became one over-night! I never even applied for it. That, too, was a God thing.

When the school board decided on a public relations person, I didn't even know about it until they told me that I had the job. Again, no application was completed. Just another level that God thought I needed.

Then, when I retired and moved to Hamilton, Texas, the phone would ring and former associates and friends would ask me to come speak and encourage their staffs or uplift their meetings. Again, God had a plan.

Today, I've spoken in almost all fifty states, have given hundreds of speeches, and none of them were ever solicited. They come from "word of mouth," and personal recommendation from folks who have been in the audience.

Now, you tell me that's not a God thing!

And now, in the autumn of my life, another book! My neighbor Dennis Ensor was the catalyst for this one. He said it would be easy, and indeed he was right!

As scripture says, "In all thy ways acknowledge Him, and He will direct your path." He certainly has directed mine, although I certainly haven't deserved it.

What a loving God we serve whose Grace is unimaginable.

So, let me encourage you. When you are asked to go a direction you might never have chosen, remember, it could be Him "directing" your path.

My thoughts and prayers are for each of you who read this book, that you will laugh, that your heart will periodically be touched, and that you will be encouraged to take a path you never dreamed possible.

Because, I believe, that my writing of this book, and your reading of this book, is a God thing, you know.

Until next time, I remain,

Your friend,

Riney

Made in the USA
Charleston, SC
27 June 2016